NOW YOU CAN READ ABOUT....

FARMS

Written by Marjorie Rogers

Illustrated by Tony Gibbons

BRIMAX BOOKS • NEWMARKET • ENGLAND

There are many kinds of farms.
Some farms keep herds of cattle.
Some farms keep sheep or pigs.
Some have no animals. On
these farms, all kinds of crops
are grown.

The farmer sells grain to be made into flour. The flour is made into bread.

This is a small farm. This farmer grows crops and keeps some animals.

There are many buildings on this farm. The tall building is called a silo. It is used to store grain and food for the animals. There is a shed where cows are milked.

Each cow has a stall and a manger for food. Pigs are kept in a shed. It is called a piggery. There are buildings to store machines and large barns to store hay.

The farmer needs to have a tractor. The tractor's engine gives the power to pull, lift and drive many kinds of machines. It pulls the plough to turn the soil over ready for sowing and planting. It can tow machines which drill, roll and bale the crops.

Here is a tractor with a crane fitted to its frame. The crane can pick up heavy logs and load them on to a truck.

Machines are used on farms all over the world. They are called by different names. They are a great help to farmers.

This farmer gets the land ready to sow barley and wheat. He uses his tractor. If the soil is heavy, he fits a harrow to the tractor to break up the earth.

To sow the seeds in rows, he uses a drill. The drill is pulled by the tractor.

This farmer plants sugar beet, potatoes and turnips. The tractor pulls a potato planter. This machine digs into the earth to make rows. It drops the seed potatoes into the rows and covers them up with earth. You can see how machines help the farmer.

In early summer, the farmer cuts the grass in the fields. Grass is the main food for many animals. It must be stored to feed them in the winter.

First, the farmer cuts the grass and turns it over. The sun dries it. Then it is called hay.

Hay is put into a baler, driven by the tractor. It gathers the hay and ties it into bales. The bales are loaded onto a truck and stored in a barn. Fresh grass is blown by a harvester into a trailer. It is put into the silo for the winter.

The corn is ready to be cut.
It is harvest time. The farmer
uses a very large machine. It is
called a combine harvester.

It has cutters which clip off the stalks. The grains from the stalks drop into a tank. The grain is taken to be dried and stored.

Some sheep farms are very big. On hill farms, dogs like this collie, look after and keep the sheep together.

There are many cows on a dairy farm. To give milk, the cow must have a calf every year. Cows eat grass and in summer, live in the fields.

The sow has many piglets. They live in a pen. The farmer will sell the piglets when they grow bigger.

This farmer keeps horses. They need lots of hay, oats and straw. The stable must be kept clean.

In spring, the sheep are taken to have their thick, woolly coats cut. This is called shearing. A machine is used to do this. The sheep's coat is cut off all in one piece. We use wool to make warm clothes and blankets.

Machines are used to milk cows. The cows are milked twice a day. Then, a tanker takes the milk away to the dairy. The dairy makes the milk ready for us to drink. Milk is used to make butter, cheese and many good things to eat.

This farmer is looking after his chickens.

He puts corn for them into hoppers. The young hens are called pullets. They will soon lay eggs. The farmer will take the eggs to sell at the market.

A very large beef cattle farm is called a ranch.

The animals will be sold for meat. Men on horseback herd or round-up the cattle. They are called cowboys or stockmen.

Can you name these?